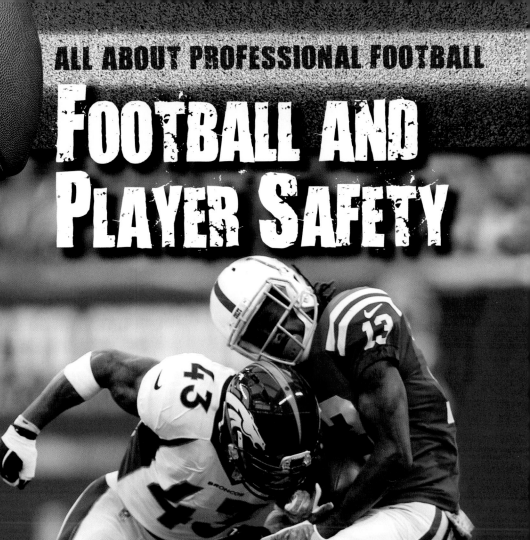

ALL ABOUT PROFESSIONAL FOOTBALL

FOOTBALL AND PLAYER SAFETY

by Phil Barber

FOOTBALL AND PLAYER SAFETY

by Phil Barber

Mason Crest
450 Parkway Drive, Suite D
Broomall, PA 19008
www.masoncrest.com

Printed and bound in the United States of America.

Series ISBN: 978-1-4222-3576-8
Hardback ISBN: 978-1-4222-3578-2
EBook ISBN: 978-1-4222-8301-1

First printing
1 3 5 7 9 8 6 4 2

Produced by Shoreline Publishing Group LLC
Santa Barbara, California
Editorial Director: James Buckley Jr.
Designer: Bill Madrid
Production: Sandy Gordon
www.shorelinepublishing.com

Cover photograph by Joe Robbins.

Library of Congress Cataloging-in-Publication Data is on file with the Publisher.

CONTENTS

Key Icons to Look For

Words to Understand: These words with their easy-to-understand definitions will increase the reader's understanding of the text, while building vocabulary skills.

Sidebars: This boxed material within the main text allows readers to build knowledge, gain insights, explore possibilities, and broaden their perspectives by weaving together additional information to provide realistic and holistic perspectives.

Educational Videos: Readers can view videos by scanning our QR codes, providing them with additional educational content to supplement the text. Examples include news coverage, moments in history, speeches, iconic sports moments, and much more!

Text-Dependent Questions: These questions send the reader back to the text for more careful attention to the evidence presented here.

Research Projects: Readers are pointed toward areas of further inquiry connected to each chapter. Suggestions are provided for projects that encourage deeper research and analysis.

Series Glossary of Key Terms: This back-of-the-book glossary contains terminology used throughout this series. Words found here increase the reader's ability to read and comprehend higher-level books and articles in this field.

INTRODUCTION

NFL stars Robert Griffin III and Richard Sherman know first hand the risks of pro football.

DECISION TIME

Washington quarterback Robert Griffin III was putting the final touches on a fairly brilliant rookie season. Griffin, who has a winning smile and a catchy nickname in "RG3," was leading the Redskins in a NFC Wild-Card playoff game against the Seattle Seahawks.

But all was not right. Griffin had sprained his right knee during in a game two weeks earlier. That injury had only cost him one game, however. But as he tried to scramble in the first quarter against the Seahawks, Griffin appeared to hurt the knee again. He went to the bench and backup quarterback Kirk Cousins trotted into the huddle.

On the sidelines, Washington coach Mike Shanahan was faced with a tough football decision. Griffin was lobbying hard to get back in the game. If he were healthy enough to play, the dynamic quarter-back would almost certainly give his team its best chance to advance through the postseason.

But RG3 wasn't just a popular young player. The second overall pick in the draft, he was a major investment for the Redskins. Was it worth risking future injury to get him back on the field for this important moment?

Shanahan decided it was. Griffin returned to action, but he looked hindered by the knee. And with 6:19 left in the game, the worst happened—he buckled in pain while trying to retrieve a low snap from his center.

Griffin had torn a knee ligament that he had injured earlier. He would undergo surgery three days later, and the consequences would extend in wide ripples. Griffin, hampered by injuries ever since, has struggled to regain the form he showed as a rookie. Shanahan would be fired after that 2013 season, in large part for the handling of his quarterback.

Though the details always vary, this is a story that many National Football League players, coaches and executives can relate to. The very qualities that have made football the most popular sport in America—the remarkable size and athleticism of the players, and the controlled violence of the action—make the game risky to play.

Each week during the NFL regular season, injury reports distributed by the 32 teams include dozens, even hundreds of banged-up players. Some of them have nothing more than a minor calf strain or a 24-hour flu bug. For others, the situation is much more serious. Shoulder separations and broken legs can ruin seasons. Recurring knee injuries or repeated concussions can prematurely end a player's career.

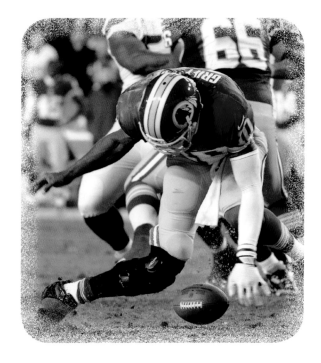

Injuries are football's wild cards. In addition to the human toll they take on athletes and their families, they can tilt the competitive balance and test a team's long-term planning. The NFL has dealt with this dilemma since it was founded as the American Professional Football Association in 1920 (trivia time: It was renamed as the NFL in 1922). But the issue

Griffin's knee buckled after he went back into the game. Was it worth the risk?

Football causes injuries at all levels of the game, from pee-wee to the pros.

of player safety has started to receive much more attention in recent years, both within the league and from fans, media members, and critics.

Of course it isn't just NFL athletes who deal with injuries. College players, high school players, even those in youth leagues such as Pop Warner and Pee Wee get hurt. It's a huge issue for schools and parents, and the culture of football definitely is changing. We're all learning that it's no longer okay to say a kid "got dinged" or "got his bell rung," and then send him back onto the field.

At every level, leagues and associations have altered the rules to make football safer, while also seeking out new technology for monitoring and pro-tective equipment.

All in all, it's fair to say the sport of football has never devoted as much time and energy to keeping its players safe as it does today. Players wear state-of-the-art helmets and pads and receive instruction on safe technique. On-site trainers and medical staff oversee an athlete's every move at the higher tiers, and even at the youth level in many cases.

Yet many wonder if it's enough.

Thanks to year-round conditioning and improved diet, each generation of players gets bigger and stronger. In effect, football players have been engineered for maximum physical impact, and their bodies pay the price for it.

The question is whether things like rules changes and technology can remove some of the risk from the game. The NFL and all the leagues that feed into it want to give their fans the action they crave, while offering the players the protection they deserve. It's like a delicate tiptoe along the sideline, except the consequences are huge.

CHAPTER 1

The great Knute Rockne shows off some of the early attempts at keeping players safe: hip pads and a leather helmet.

THE FOOTBALL SAFETY STORY

Football has changed so dramatically over the past century and a half. It has changed so much that an Ivy League player from 1869 would hardly recognize the game played today, and vice versa. But one thread remains constant as the sport has evolved: This is a rough, physical activity.

While people still argue over the details, most would agree that what Americans call football has its roots in what the rest of the world calls football—the game of soccer. More than that, football was based on rugby, which was born in England in the 1820s.

Words to Understand

fail-safe describing a procedure that is a last resort in a chain of protective steps

polycarbonate a hard, synthetic, plastic-like material that is the outer shell of football helmets

scrums collections or piles of bodies in a sport, specifically rugby football

side judge the position name of one of the seven officials on the football field

Early players wore canvas pants with leather patches and sometimes with wooden slats on the thighs.

Like rugby, early football involved carrying or kicking the ball (which sort of looked like a leather watermelon), and involved massive "**scrums**" or piles of bodies. There weren't nearly as many of the high-speed collisions we see today. But with almost no protective padding, the game offered plenty of pounding, elbowing, and eye gouging.

Here's an account of an 1893 football game between rivals Harvard and Yale, as reported in a German newspaper:

"It turned into an awful butchery. Of twenty-two participants, seven were so severely injured that they had to be carried from the field in a dying condition. One player had his back broken, another lost an eye, and a third lost a leg. Both teams appeared upon the field with a crown of ambulances, surgeons and nurses. Many ladies fainted at the awful cries of the injured players."

By 1905, college football had grown highly popular, especially on the East Coast. And already the sport faced its first major safety-related crisis.

Teddy to the Rescue

According to the *Washington Post*, at least 45 men died from football-related injuries between 1900 and 1905, most from internal bleeding, broken necks, or head injuries. At least 18 people were killed in 1905 alone. The public outcry was huge. Columbia, Duke and Northwestern, three of America's top universities, suspended their football programs. The president of Harvard, Charles Eliot, wanted to ban the sport altogether, calling it "more brutalizing than prizefighting, cockfighting, or bullfighting."

The person credited with saving the game was U.S. President Theodore Roosevelt. He cut a rugged figure in his own right, and he was a big football fan.

"I believe in rough games and in rough, manly sports," Roosevelt told an audience in 1903. "I do not feel any particular sympathy for the person who gets battered about a good deal so long as it is not fatal."

But the President also had a son who was injured, cut badly above his eye, while playing as a freshman at Harvard.

Moved by the experience, Roosevelt twice met with coaches and athletic advisors from several major colleges, including Harvard and Yale, to propose rules changes. The new rules included stopping the game when a player fell on the ball, and allowing for forward passes. Today, many of football's most dangerous plays involve downfield passes to vulnerable receivers. At the time, the forward pass spread the field and reduced the violence in the scrums.

When the NFL was formed in 1920 (it was called the APFA for its first two seasons), pro football adopted most of the rules of college football. For most of its history, though, the NFL has led the way in modifying the rulebook, including the parts dealing with player safety.

Rules to Protect Players

Some elements of the NFL rulebook have evolved gradually. The dangerous crackback block, where a player lined up outside runs parallel to the line of scrimmage and hits an unsuspecting defender below the waist, is banned. Since it was introduced in the 1970s, the no-crackback rule has been extended to more players, and to a wider area.

Another example: striking a "defenseless player." Since 1982, this rule has expanded to include more ways of hitting an opponent and, especially, the pool of players considered defenseless. It now refers to kickoff and punt returners attempting to field a kick in the air, players on the ground at the end of plays, placekickers and punters in the act of kicking, a quarterback during change of possession, a receiver who hasn't had time to protect himself, and a receiver after a pass is intercepted.

The tinkering never stops. In 2015, among other safety measures, NFL owners authorized injury spot-

Football receivers are particularly vulnerable to hard hits as they focus first on making the catch.

Rules Changes

Here is a brief and incomplete list of safety-related rules added or changed through the years:

1938: "Unnecessary roughness" against a quarterback after the ball leaves his hand is prohibited.

1956: Grabbing the facemask of an opponent is ruled illegal and assessed a 5-yard penalty.

1977: The head slap used by defensive linemen is outlawed entirely.

1979: The quarterback is ruled down when clearly "in the grasp" of a defender.

2005: The horse-collar tackle, or grabbing the inside collar of the shoulder pads to drag down a runner, is prohibited.

2009: Teams are no longer permitted to form a "wedge" of two or more blockers on kickoff returns.

ters to stop a game when a player appears to have suffered a head injury.

The league already had certified athletic trainers positioned in booths overseeing the action on the field. Now, if the spotter sees a clearly injured player remaining in the game he can alert the official known as the **side judge**, who immediately passes along the information to the player's medical staff. The play clock freezes.

"We do not expect this to be a rule that gets used a lot," said Rich McKay, Atlanta Falcons president and chairman of the NFL Competition Committee. "We expect it to be a **fail-safe** when people just don't see this player and the distress the player may have had, the spotter does and stops the game."

The NCAA, as well as high school leagues and school districts all over the United States, have contributed to player safety, too. But usually change has come from the top down. It's natural for amateurs to look to professionals for guidance. And there's another important reason: Since 1956, the NFL has had a players' union to represent its athletes and advocate for their safety. Because college and high school players aren't considered employees (not yet, anyway; some collegiate athletes are attempting to gain that status), they must rely on others to make the game safe for them.

Pro and college teams provide experts to help players prepare to play the game and deal with injuries after.

Equipment and Safety

There is another major aspect of football safety, and that is equipment. Like the rules of the game, the gear worn by its players has changed dramatically over the years.

In 1877, a Princeton University student named L.P. Smock stitched pads made of wool and leather into players' jerseys. These were the forerunners of modern shoulder pads. A larger, harnessed version, slipped over the head, was introduced in the early 1900s. Much later, in the 1960s, we started to see the plastic shoulder pads most football fans are familiar with.

The most obvious and significant equipment innovation is the football helmet. Its origin is usually traced to 1893, when Joseph Mason Reeve, determined to play in the Army-Navy game despite getting hit in the head so many times his doctor worried another blow could lead to "instant insanity," had a shoemaker design a moleskin hat with earflaps.

It wasn't a lot of protection, but it was a start. By the early 1900s most college players were wearing soft leather headgear, and by the 1920s, when pioneers like Red Grange and Curly Lambeau were building NFL popularity, players had begun to switch to hard leather models. The chinstrap was introduced in 1939.

Amazingly, the NFL didn't make helmets mandatory until 1943. Six years after that, the league adopted plastic helmets for the first time, dramatically changing the game. John T. Riddell had introduced the concept a decade earlier, but it took a while to perfect the technology.

Then came logos, facemasks (starting with a single Lucite bar in 1955, devised by the Cleveland Browns to protect quarterback Otto Graham) and, in the 1970s, air bladders that the Riddell company added to serve as shock absorbers upon impact. In the 1980s, the company began making helmets that featured an outer shell of **polycarbonate** over a layer of aluminum and vinyl foam over a layer of plastic over a thin layer of leather. In the late 1990s, some players began to add transparent plastic visors to protect their eyes.

It may come as a surprise that there is little in the NFL rule book to govern helmets. The only real guideline is that they must be approved by the National Operating

Football Helmet of the Future
Puts Safety First

Helmets continue to evolve, adding new layers of padding, masks, straps, and more.

Committee on Standards for Athletic Equipment, or NOCSAE.

The evolution of the football helmet presents a riddle, though. As they have become more protective—if you were in a motorcycle accident, would you rather wear a helmet made of soft leather or molded polycarbonate?—the players who wear them have become more comfortable using them for impact.

In the days of Bronko Nagurski, players didn't lead with their helmets when tackling. It hurt too much. Today, players feel relatively invulnerable. As we will see, they are anything but that.

 Text-Dependent Questions

1. From what two sports does the text say football evolved?

2. What type of player was protected with the 1982 rule about hitting them?

3. Name the man credited with perfecting hard-helmet technology.

 Research Project

Read about the different makes and models of football helmets. List their materials, weights, and protective qualities. Which one would you choose to wear if you were playing football?

CHAPTER 2

In the NFL team doctors, trainers, and coaches all have responsibilities for helping keep players safe.

The Safety Team

Professional football is a cruel business. Young players, especially those who were not drafted in a high round, get few chances to redeem mistakes. Teams will release athletes as soon as they lose value, no matter how much service they have provided to the organization.

But that's not to say the NFL doesn't surround its talent with a large support group. All drafted first-year players are required to attend the NFL Rookie **Symposium**, where they receive advice on business and life.

Words to Understand

anti-inflammatory drugs medicine used to reduce swelling, usually at the site of earlier injuries

impairment a measure of a state of not being able to function fully and normally

neurological having to do with the brain and the body's nervous system

symposium a gathering at which information is presented to and shared by participants

watchdog in this case, referring to a group that oversees the actions of an organization, looking for possible trouble

"Only a fool learns from his own mistakes," former wide receiver Donte Stallworth told the rookies in 2014, as recounted by Robert Klemko for the MMQB website. "The wise man learns from the mistakes of others. Let me be your experience. Let me make the mistake. Learn it today from me, not on your own."

Stallworth served jail time for DUI manslaughter after striking a man with his car in Miami one night in 2009.

Once a player settles in with his team, he receives a level of care most Americans could only dream of. Of course, they need a lot more care than most of us. NFL players have described their games as something like experiencing a major car accident every Sunday. Their jobs are extremely physical and often punishing. And noted, each team has a huge financial incentive in keeping its players healthy throughout the season, and beyond.

Trainer!

The first line of defense in the fight to keep players physically sound is a team's training staff. These are certified athletic trainers who have specific education in the dangers of football.

Years ago, an NFL trainer taped ankles, doled out aspirin, and informally checked out players who seemed dazed. The job is way more sophisticated these days. NFL football has become nearly a year-round occupation, with players showing up for voluntary organized team activities and mandatory mini-camps in the "offseason." Many show up at the team facility most days to work out, too. All of it is overseen by the training staff.

The first line of relief for an injured player is a certified athletic trainer.

Trainers still tape ankles and give out painkillers and **anti-inflammatory drugs**, but they do much more. They counsel players on icing and heating their muscles, on stretching exercises, on staying hydrated, on recognizing the difference between something that hurts and a true injury that shouldn't be played through.

"We take care of everything from the common cold to a torn ACL [anterior cruciate ligament, a key part of the knee] to a ruptured spleen to getting players with depression a proper referral," Geoff Kaplan, the head athletic trainer of the Houston Texans, told the Milwaukee Journal Sentinel. "Our job as athletic trainer is prevention of injuries, assessment and evaluation of injuries, and rehabilitation."

One of the trainers' most important functions is to oversee recovery from injuries. Every injury is different, and each player is unique. It takes a trained eye and solid data to figure out the right time to return to practice or to game action. Members of the training staff monitor the recovery. For each player and each injury, they design the proper exercises for the best rehab. They even help athletes deal with the psychological hardship of the process.

Beyond the Trainer

The care isn't limited to trainers. Pretty much every NFL team has a staff chiropractor to keep players' spines aligned and a nutritionist to make sure they're getting what they need to refuel, and some are working with acupuncturists and other specialists. Professional athletes are better educated about their bodies now, too, and often seek their own forms of treatment after clearing it with their teams.

Despite all these caretakers, injuries still happen. Lots of injuries. When they do occur, a player is referred to a team doctor. Generally, these doctors have private practices away from the football field. But they are on the sidelines, in some combination, for all games and practices, in case an emergency should arise. The Oakland Raiders' 2015 media guide listed a team medical physician, a team orthopedist, an orthopedic consultant, and two medical consultants. All of them are doctors.

In addition, teams have relationships with local hospitals should a player need serious medical care. For example, if a linebacker hurts his shoulder

Along with helping athletes recover from injuries, trainers work to make sure the players are ready to play.

at practice and the severity of the injury isn't immediately clear, he will probably be sent to a medical center to receive an MRI, which is sort of like a 3D X-ray that shows muscles and ligaments as well as bones.

According to the 2015 NFL Health & Safety Report, the average NFL game includes 27 health providers to help oversee the players' welfare. That includes everyone from primary care physicians to a radiology technician to a dentist. The league has various **watchdog** groups like the Head, Neck and Spine Committee, the Cardiovascular Health Subcommittee, and the Foot and Ankle Subcommittee.

More Needed in High School

The NFL has the advantage of being a financial giant, which explains this thorough degree of healthcare. Unfortunately, athletes can't always expect the equivalent at lower levels of play.

At a major university football program like Alabama or Ohio State, athletes can expect care to match the NFL's. Some of those schools offer degrees in the field of athletic training, meaning a steady supply of college-age interns. As you work your way down the football chain, though, the budgets get smaller, and so do the staffs. Every college team has a trainer, but the players might not get as much individual attention.

The real issue is at the high school level. Healthcare professionals have been arguing for some time that every school should have at least one certified athletic trainer present for all contact sports (which include games like soccer and baseball). In 2013, the National Athletic Trainers' Association stated that about 55 percent of U.S. high schools were so equipped. That was up from about 40 percent just a few years before, a positive trend.

Still, it's safe to say that many schools around the country have no trainer on campus, or even one on game night. If a player gets hurt in a football game, it would fall to the coaches to diagnose the injury, unless a doctor just happened to be watching from the stands.

Nutrition, Hydration & Health—
Science of NFL Football

To many in the medical field, this is unacceptable. The Youth Sports Safety Alliance released a list of 40 fatalities in high school and youth sports in 2012. Most of them were related to heart failure. Meanwhile, according to research presented at the American Academy of Pediatrics National Conference in 2012, athletes at schools with full-time athletic trainers had lower rates of both overall injury and recurring injury. Schools around the country are starting to pay attention and devote budget and time to the problem, but it is far from solved.

The Problem of Concussions

If the resources vary greatly between, say, the Miami Dolphins and your local public high school, the current hot-button issue is the same. That's because over the past decade, more and more attention has focused on one particular health concern associated with football. It's a problem that results in short-term pain and mental **impairment**. Even worse, a growing body of research suggests it can have dire long-term effects that include dementia, depression and **neurological** issues. Some would go so far as to say it's killing our football heroes.

The problem is concussions.

Bill Romanowski knows all about them. "Romo" was a feared and decorated linebacker for 16 NFL seasons. He played in five Super Bowls with three different teams, and won four of them. And while many people questioned his sportsmanship and occasionally his sanity as he argued and fought with opponents, no one ever doubted Romanowski's football intelligence.

Yet in his final weeks as a player, he suffered several mental lapses that scored him. "I left the Raider parking lot two weeks before I retired, and I couldn't find my home," Romanowski told the (Santa Rosa, California) Press Democrat in 2010. "A drive I made every day. It was ten minutes away from the

Former NFL linebacker Bill Romanowski knows well the dangers posed by concussions.

Raider facility. I just kept driving. It took a half-hour, but it finally came to me. I was too scared to call my wife and ask her. I was just kind of in this daze."

Romanowski was a victim of repeated concussions. He figures he had more than 20 during his football career. Brain researchers might argue he had more than that, because the definition of "concussion" is becoming broader all the time.

One thing is certain: Romanowski is not the only football player to be laid low by head injuries. Just about every veteran NFL player has stories of absorbing hits that made their thoughts fuzzy. So do many college players, and even high school athletes.

The issue has drawn the attention of parents everywhere. "I'm a big football fan," one citizen told the *New Republic* magazine, "but I have to tell you, if I had a son I'd have to think long and hard before I let him play football." The speaker was Barack Obama, the President of the United States.

Text-Dependent Questions

1. What is the name of the event at which new NFL players are advised about health and wellness?

2. Which level of football has the best access to medical care?

3. What is the biggest health issue facing football?

 Research Project

For your favorite NFL or college team, go online and find the complete list of their medical personnel. What specialties are included? Or read an interview with an NFL team doctor to find out more about what they do to help players.

CHAPTER 3

Chicago Bears quarterback Jay Cutler suffered a concussion on this play, one of many that NFL players deal with each year.

THE CONCUSSION QUESTION

The more we know, the more we realize that concussions are the most dangerous health risk in football—and the biggest threat to the game's existence.

The basic definition of a concussion, according to the Mayo Clinic, is "a **traumatic** brain injury that alters the way your brain functions." Frequently a concussion is caused by a strong blow to the head, but they can also occur when the head and upper body are violently shaken, causing the brain to bang against the inside of the skull.

Words to Understand

cognitive having to do with thinking or human mental processes

dementia a medical condition in which the brain breaks down, resulting in lower and lower mental function

deteriorates breaks down over time

posthumously occurring after a person's death

traumatic in medicine, describing an injury that is very significant, resulting in damage to body tissues

The classic concussion involves loss of consciousness, but it's clear now that this isn't always the case. Symptoms can include headaches, nausea, memory loss, and problems with concentration, balance, and coordination.

Doctors have known about concussions for ages, and it has never been a secret that a football game is a particularly likely place for them to happen. It's a game with vicious collisions and a warrior mentality.

The Hits Add Up

"I don't want to come out of games. I always feel that's some kind of weakness," New Orleans Saints defensive lineman Anthony Hargrove told the Associated Press. "Somebody hits me and takes me out of the game, I feel weak. So if something happens, I take a minute to try to regather myself and then go back."

During his Hall of Fame career, Steve Young took some serious hits.

With the last generation of players, and the current one, serving as unwitting test cases, we have learned that head injuries are far more dangerous than once thought.

The real problem is not the dramatic knockout hit that sends a player to the sidelines for smelling salts, though of course those are cause for concern. It's the cumulative effect of repeated head injuries, including smaller ones that players might not even recognize as concussions.

"Looking at what's happened and kind of taking it in its holistic view, the thing I fear most for players in football is what they're calling the micro-concussions, these things that happen daily, the things that you don't even necessarily notice—practices, games, linemen, running backs, linebackers, just the nature of the game," former NFL quarterback Steve Young, whose career was ended by concussions, told the PBS investigative program "Frontline." "Not violent hits, because those make ESPN."

Unfortunately, it has taken some horribly dramatic events to drive the issue home.

The Sad Results

The first high-profile NFL player to publicly suffer from mental ailments was probably Mike Webster, the Pro Football Hall of Fame center who won four Super Bowl rings with the Pittsburgh Steelers of the 1970s. Late in his life, Webster lived out of his car and struggled to manage his personal affairs.

It was hard to watch, but people could dismiss Webster as an isolated example. Maybe he had mental problems that would have developed with or without football.

More recent cases have shot holes in that theory. Dave Duerson was not only a starting safety for some great Chicago Bears defenses in the late 1980s, he was a charming and intelligent man who had political aspirations. Duerson shot himself in the heart in 2011. Jovan Belcher wasn't as well known as Duerson. But he was younger, just 24 years old, in 2012 when he shot his girlfriend, then himself.

The death that struck home with most NFL fans, though, was the suicide of former linebacker Junior Seau in May of 2012. Seau played 17 seasons in the league, most with the San Diego Chargers and was considered one of the best defenders of his generation. In fact, he was elected to the Pro Football Hall of Fame **posthumously** in 2015. He was tough, fiery, full of life. But he, too, shot himself in the chest.

"He would sometimes lose his temper," Seau's son Tyler told ESPN. "He would get irritable over very small things. And he would take it out on not just myself but also other people that he was close to. And I didn't understand why."

NFL + CTE

After autopsies, all of these players were diagnosed with something called chronic traumatic encephalopathy, better known as CTE. NFL is a three-letter acronym, and so is the physical condition that now threatens its popularity.

Encephalopathy comes from ancient Greek words that translate to "suffering in the head," and

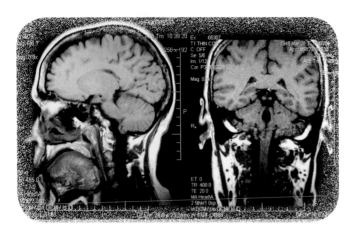

Brain scans like this one can prove a vital tool in diagnosing short-term and long-term brain injuries.

CTE describes a condition in which the brain **deteriorates** over a period of years or decades because of repeated blows to the head.

Doctors can spot CTE in brains they examine after a person's death. Some areas of the brain are likely to atrophy, or shrivel, when the person suffers from CTE, while others become enlarged. The condition seems to be related to a build-up of something called "tau protein," which can interfere with the firing of neurons, the little electrical switches that control our brain function.

If the causes of CTE are complicated, the symptoms are all too clear. According to the website of the Brain Injury Research Institute, "Some of the most common include loss of memory, difficulty controlling impulsive or erratic behavior, impaired judgment, behavioral disturbances including aggression and depression, difficulty with balance, and a gradual onset of **dementia**."

The institute's home page includes a photograph of Mike Webster in his Steelers uniform.

As dementia sets in, the CTE patient may have trouble recognizing loved ones or separating reality from fantasy. It's painful to watch, frustrating for the victim and terrifying for his or her family.

In recent years, the news has been filled with additional research findings, with head injuries linked to disorders like Parkinson's disease, Alzheimer's disease and ALS, also known as Lou Gehrig's disease.

Former football players continue to struggle with their mental function, though not all of them wind up making headlines. Many of them live in quiet pain and confusion, searching for treatments that will relieve their symptoms.

Early Diagnosis

Medical researchers first diagnosed CTE in boxers. In fact, they used to call it *dementia pugilistica*–pugilism is another word for boxing. In 2002, two doctors affiliated with the Brain Injury Research Institute became the first to diagnose the disorder in a pro football player when they examined Mike Webster's brain. One of those physicians, Bennet Omalu, was the subject of the 2015 movie *Concussion*.

It's Not Just the Pros

Of course, not all concussion sufferers are professional athletes. In 2010, Dr. Ann McKee, working with a group of researchers at Boston University, reported the first case of CTE in a college football player. Owen Thomas, a defensive end and team captain at the University of Pennsylvania, hanged himself at his apartment at the age of 21, and was found to have the telltale signs of brain trauma.

Thomas' case was particularly scary because, according to his family, he had never been diagnosed with a concussion. His case shed light on "subconcussive collisions," smaller blows that can, after many repetitions, add up to a serious problem.

And the news seems only to be getting worse. A Boston University School of Medicine study of former NFL players published in 2015 indicated that those who played tackle football between the ages of 10 and 12 were more likely to struggle with **cognitive** functions like memory, reasoning, and planning, as well being more susceptible to depression. In other words, the sport is starting to seem unsafe at any age.

Parents and schools have noticed. In June of 2015, the Maplewood Richmond Heights School

Board, in a suburb of St. Louis, voted to disband the local high school football team—a team that had reached the Missouri state championship game five years earlier.

"Over all, it was, 'Can we field a team that is competitive and safe for the kids to perform?'" said Nelson Mitten, the school board president.

The answer, apparently, was no.

The impact of concussions on young players is changing how the game is played and coached.

Admitting the Problem

Part of football's concussion problem is a culture that praises athletes for their toughness and willingness to "take one for the team," and penalizes them for missing practice time or games.

Seattle Seahawks cornerback Richard Sherman, who was educated at Stanford and would certainly have career choices beyond football, wrote a guest column for the football website MMQB.com in which he admitted to playing his first NFL game

Even a "tough" player like Richard Sherman understands the dangers of repeated concussions.

(in 2011) while suffering from the effects of a concussion.

"I couldn't see," Sherman wrote. "The concussion blurred my vision and I played the next two quarters half-blind, but there was no way I was coming off the field with so much at stake. It paid off: Just as my head was clearing, [Cincinnati Bengals quarterback] Andy Dalton lobbed one up to rookie A.J. Green and I came down with my first career interception."

But if today's players have been clued in to the dangers of head injuries and must accept much of the responsibility for taking the risk, it's much harder to place that burden on the players who came before.

And that is precisely the thinking behind a series of lawsuits that have, or will, cost the NFL hundreds of millions of dollars, and that threaten to rage on the airwaves for years to come.

The legal action started in 2011 when former Atlanta Falcons safety Ray Easterling sued the league, claiming it had made a "concerted effort of deception and denial" in the way it handled concussion research. Other retired players began to sign on. Eventually, more than 5,000 were suing the NFL.

Their basic claim was that the league had knowingly hidden or overlooked evidence that head injuries were affecting veteran players. Certainly there was a time, years ago, when no one understood the science of concussions very well. And it would be hard to claim that the NFL isn't doing quite a bit to educate and protect its players now. But there was a transition period, the retired players insisted, when the league lied to its athletes.

And indeed, for a 15-year period beginning in 1994, the NFL consistently denied the widespread or long-term harm of concussions.

During this time, the league's views on the topic were usually announced by a group formed by then-Commissioner Paul Tagliabue in 1994, the Mild Traumatic Brain Injury (MTBI) committee. Even the name seems wrong now. The chairs of that committee between 1994 and 2009, Dr. Elliot Pellman and Dr. Ira Casson, went to great lengths to downplay the risk of head injury in football.

"Concussions, I think, is one of these pack journalism issues, frankly," Tagliabue said in 1994, as highlighted in an episode of the PBS series "Frontline." "There is no increase in concussions, the number is relatively small....The problem is a journalist issue."

Evidence to the contrary began mounting through the 2000s, as doctors like Omalu and McKee demonstrated stronger connections between football and CTE, and found more and more players who suffered from brain damage when they died. But the NFL refused to acknowledge the research. In fact, the MTBI began to submit its own studies to scientific journals like Neurology.

NFL's Roger Goodell on Concussions

The Settlement

Eventually, the piles of evidence were too strong to deny. Roger Goodell was elected commissioner in 2006, and within three years the NFL had changed its stance.

"It's quite obvious from the medical research that's been done that concussions can lead to long-term problems," a league spokesman said in December of 2009. It marked the first time the NFL had made such a concession.

But that's different than admitting guilt, and the lawsuits made their way through the courts. Finally, in August of 2013, the NFL agreed to pay $765 million to settle with former players. Federal judge Anita Brody felt that wasn't enough. She encouraged the two sides to revise the settlement, and on Apr. 22, 2015, she approved a landmark deal that some believe will eventually pay out more than $1 billion to players who retired before July 7, 2014.

The agreement provides up to $5 million each to players who are diagnosed with one of several

NFL Commissioner Roger Goodell faced tough questions during the league's struggle to find an acceptable agreement for helping former players.

neurological disorders, plus additional medical monitoring for all players, as well as $10 million for education about concussions.

Even that isn't necessarily the end of the matter, though. More than 200 retirees chose not to take the settlement. Their main complaint was that it provided money for players with ailments like Parkinson's and ALS, but said nothing about CTE. It also failed to address mood disorders. These claims threatened to stall payment to eligible players, creating the possibility of a conflict between different groups of retired athletes.

"What matters now is time, and many retired players do not have much left," Kevin Turner, a retired running back suffering from ALS, told *The New York Times*. "I hope this settlement is implemented without delay so that we can finally start helping those in need."

Soon after that, though, nearly 100 former players filed about a dozen appeals.

In March 2016, Jeff Miller, the NFL's senior vice president for health and safety, appeared before a Congressional panel. For the first time publicly, the

NFL, in the person of Miller, admitted a direct link between concussions and CTE. It was seen as a turning point in the fight to find a solution. Still, while there is widespread agreement on the biology and chemistry, as an issue of debate, concussions aren't going away anytime soon.

 # Text-Dependent Questions

　　1. What are some of the symptoms of concussions?

　　2. Name one of the NFL players listed in the text who committed.

　　3. Describe how CTE harms players' brains.

 # Research Project

　　Talk to your doctor or school athletic trainer about how to recognize the signs of concussions. Or talk to football players at your school about whether they have ever suffered one, and if so, what it felt like. What are the school policies on concussions?

CHAPTER 4

Hits like this one scared Chris Borland enough that he left
behind his NFL career and millions of dollars.

THE FUTURE OF FOOTBALL SAFETY

We seem to have reached an uncertain stage in the evolution of football safety. While debating the details, most players, coaches, executives, fans, and analysts would agree on an important point: Football is a dangerous game. We need to do everything we can, within reason, to take care of its athletes.

How do we achieve that? The science of head trauma and sports injuries has gotten ahead of the science of protection and recovery.

Chris Borland, for one, doesn't believe tackle football can be played safely. Borland, a tough inside linebacker, had a fantastic rookie year for the San Francisco 49ers in 2014, averaging better than 12.6 tackles per game after taking over midseason for an injured team-

Words to Understand

assessment the process of looking at evidence to arrive at a conclusion

protocol in this instance, a pre-planned series of steps or tests undertaken by medical professionals working with players

mate. In 2015, Borland shocked the 49ers, and NFL fans everywhere, when he announced his retirement after the season at the age of 24, citing his concern over head injuries.

Borland told *ESPN the Magazine,* "The game may be safer; you can make an argument about that. My experience over my five years at Wisconsin and my one year in the NFL was that there were times where I couldn't play the game safely."

Not surprisingly, much of the current energy is focused on concussions—how to evaluate them, how to prevent them, how to treat them.

Can Testing Help?

Baseline testing, a computer-based system that measures an athlete's powers of memory, concentration, and problem solving, is offered by several companies.

The Concussion Vital Signs program is an example. Before the beginning of a season, and under normal, healthy conditions, each athlete logs on to a Web site and takes a series of quick cognitive tests. In one segment, the program randomly generates 15 words and flashes them on the screen, one by one; the participant then has to identify those words nested among 15 new words. Another section records how many times an athlete can tap the Space bar with his or her right index finger in 10 seconds. Responses are measured by the millisecond. The entire test takes about 45 minutes.

The idea is get a snapshot of the subject's brain function. Later, if it's suspected that an athlete might have suffered a head injury, he or she retakes the test, and the results are measured against the original to see if the person is impaired in any way.

The baseline test does not diagnose a concussion. But it's an important piece of evidence a doctor can use to make that **assessment**, and it takes some of the pressure off of trainers and coaches who have to explain their decisions to athletes or parents.

Baseline testing is especially important at the high school level, and not just for football but for all contact sports. Public schools don't always have the resources for one-on-one medical care. For a small fee, a campus can test all of its athletes.

When Is It Safe to Return?

Of course, testing is just part of the solution. Equally vital is coming up with the proper "return to play" standards. Most teams, whether at the high school level or in the NFL, having a minimum rest period for any player who suffers a head injury. That player can't return until he completes a predetermined concussion **protocol**, and must be cleared by a doctor.

Maybe most important of all, the culture of football is gradually changing, becoming more intelligent and less macho. In the past, when a player rose from a pile looking wobbly and confused, people would say he got "dinged" or "got his bell rung." It was treated lightly, and the athlete would frequently be sent back into the game as soon as his head had cleared a bit.

Now we know better. A rung bell is a head injury, and must be taken seriously.

Also, at the prep-football level, schools are realizing the advantage of having a certified athletic trainer on campus, and especially at games. Things like baseline testing are valuable only if a trained professional is there to interpret the results.

Is the NFL Doing Enough?

Whether or not you believe the league was slow to react to news about concussions, it has clearly made strides to identify and prevent them in the past few years.

In December of 2009, for example, the NFL announced stricter return-to-play guidelines, stating that any player exhibiting symptoms should not come back the same day. The league's Head, Neck and Spine Committee has a five-step return-to-participation process. It begins with rest and recovery, and progresses through light aerobic exercise, strength training, and football-specific activities before a player is cleared for football activity.

In the summer of 2010, the league instructed all 32 teams to hang posters in their locker rooms. The posters read, in part, "Concussions and conditions resulting from repeated brain injury can change your life and your family's life forever."

In February of 2015, the NFL hired Dr. Elizabeth Nabel, the president of Brigham and Women's Hospital and a professor of

The NFL Needs to Evolve to Protect Players

HEADS UP!

Knowing that football safety starts with the youngest players, the NFL has connected with youth leagues through the Heads Up Football initiative. This program educates kids on things like hydration, sudden cardiac arrest, and wearing equipment correctly, in addition to concussions. Most important, Heads Up Football focuses on proper tackling and blocking technique. Many serious injuries can be avoided if players use the right form when tackling—head and eyes up, striking with the front of the shoulder and driving upward—instead of leading with the crown of the helmet. More than 6,000 leagues and high schools have signed on, benefiting upward of 1 million players.

medicine at Harvard Medical School, as its chief medical advisor.

The NFL and its players have also made an effort to fund medical study. The league donated $30 million to the National Institutes of Health for research into brain trauma in 2010, and the NFLPA, the players' union, gave $100 million to Harvard Medical School in 2013 for a wide range of studies.

The NFL insists that its policies are working to make the game safer. The 2015 NFL Health & Safety Report noted that since 2012, concussions in regular-season games are down 35 percent and concussions caused by helmet-to-helmet hits are down 43 percent,. According to the NFL, there were 112 concussions during the 2014 season, fewer than one-half per game. However, many quibble with the numbers. The league remains on the hot seat.

Looking at More Rule Changes

Rules changes may be part of the ongoing solution. The NFL identified kickoffs as the plays with the highest rate of injury. The league moved kickoffs from the 30-yard line to its 35 in 2011, which resulted in many more touchbacks,.

Some analysts and former players would like to completely eliminate the kickoff, which gives players half a football field to gain steam before collisions.

Hard hits on kickoff returns were identified as a source of concussions. Will the play go away?

"We'll have in fifteen years an entirely new generation of football fans that won't remember what it's like," said Steve Tasker, who covered kickoffs as well as anyone in the game during his 13 NFL seasons. "Kickoffs will probably go away, and I don't think too many people will miss it."

Technology Bring Tools

As the NFL tinkers with its rules and works to educate its players, the sport is also exploring the ways that technology can help improve safety.

In 2014, several college programs began using the Riddell SpeedFlex helmet, which flexes in key areas in an attempt to prevent impact from transferring to the athlete's head. The SpeedFlex is equipped with software that measures how violently the wearer's head moves upon impact. If it falls outside of an acceptable range, the sensors send a wireless alert to a coach or trainer on the sidelines.

Medical technology is catching up, too. Researchers affiliated with UCLA have developed a brain scan they say can find signs of CTE, and especially the buildup of tau protein, in people who are still alive. More than a dozen retired players volunteered for the scan, and they showed clear signs of damage.

Some NFL fans lament that all of this modern research has taken some of the fun out of watching. But we can't afford that sort of ignorance now, though. Football is changing, and no one is exactly sure where it's headed.

Dr. Nabel sees the NFL as a leader. She also knows the reality of the sport she now watches over.

"Football is getting safer all the time," she said. "But we have a long ways to go. It's going to be a long, hard journey."

 # Text-Dependent Questions

1. From what NFL team did Chris Borland retire out of fear of concussions?

2. Name one recent step the NFL took to call players' attention to concussions.

3. What concussion-causing play might be cut from football rules?

 # Research Project

Look at football rules and come up with three or four ideas on how they might be changed to help reduce the number of concussions.

FIND OUT MORE

Books

Laskas, Jeanne Marie. *Concussion*. New York: Random House, 2015. The book on which the movie starring Will Smith was based follows Dr. Bennett Omalu, one of the first to call attention to the concussion problem, as he battles the NFL.

McClafferty, Carla Killough. *Fourth Down and Inches: Concussions and Football's Make-or-Break Moment*. Minneapolis: Carolrhoda Books, 2013. A young-adult-level look at the issues of concussions in football at all levels.

Websites

usafootball.com/health-safety/home
A national youth football site provides safe-tackling and other health tips.

www.nflhealthplaybook.com/
Sponsored by the NFL, this site collects articles and news about football safety.

www.nata.org/brochures-and-other-informational-materials
The National Athletic Trainers' Association provides videos and online articles.

SERIES GLOSSARY OF KEY TERMS

alma mater the school that someone attended

analytics in sports, using and evaluating data beyond traditional game statistics to predict a player's future success

brass a slang term for the high-ranking executives of an organization

bundling in television, the concept of customers paying for a set of cable channels with one set fee

bye weeks the weeks that NFL teams do not play a game; each team gets one bye week per season

credentialed provided with an official pass allowing entry into a private or restricted area

eligibility in this case, the right to continue to play on a college team, granted by both the school and the NCAA

endorsement support and praise offered by a paid spokesperson for a product or service

expansion team a new franchise that starts from scratch

feedback information used to improve something

general managers members of a sports team's front office in charge of building that club's roster

leverage the ability to direct the course of action in a decision

merger to combine into one

perennial occurring or returning every year; annually

protocol in this instance, a pre-planned series of steps or tests undertaken by medical professionals working with players

public relations the process of telling the public about a product, service, or event from the "company" point of view

red zone for the team with possession of the football, the area of the field from the opponents' 20-yard line to the goal line

special teams the kicking game in football: kickoffs, punts, field goals, and extra points

traumatic in medicine, describing an injury that is very significant, resulting in damage to body tissues

INDEX

CREDITS

Dreamstime.com: Susan Leggett 10, Aspenphoto 19, Tomislav Birtic 22, Starletdarlene 40, Katrina Brown 42, James Boardman 45. Courtesy Gregg Ficery: 14. Newscom: Marc Gaile/UPI 6, Hary E. Walker/MCT 9, Rich Graessle/Icon Sportswire 17, Andrew Dieb/Icon Sportswire 24, Carlos Gonzalez/MCT 27, Doug Muray/Icon SMI 30, Jeff Carlick/Icon SMI 33, Brian Casella/MCT 36, John Cordes/Icon SMI 38, Tom Walko/Icon Sportwire 46, Chris Coduto/Icon Sportswire 49, Al Golub/Icon Sportswire DDJ 52, Jeff Siner/MCT 59.

ABOUT THE AUTHOR

Phil Barber covers the Oakland Raiders and San Francisco 49ers (and pretty much everything else) for the *Santa Rosa Press Democrat*. He is the author of more than a dozen books, including *The Vince Lombardi Playbook* and *When We Were Champions: The 49ers' Dynasty in Their Own Words*. Barber was formerly a senior editor for NFL Publishing. He writes a blog called "110 Percent" and tweets dumb things under the handle @Skinny_Post.